IMMANUEL KANT

1724-1924

IMMANUEL KANT

BY HEINRICH WOLFF

Made for the Königsberg commemorative volume,
IMMANUEL KANT,
and reproduced here by the courtesy of the publishers.

IMMANUEL KANT
1724-1924

BY

GEORGE HERBERT PALMER

MARY W. CALKINS · E. C. WILM · W. E. HOCKING

HARLOW SHAPLEY · KUNO FRANCKE

ROSCOE POUND

AND GERHART VON SCHULZE-GAEVERNITZ

EDITED BY E. C. WILM

PROFESSOR OF PHILOSOPHY IN BOSTON UNIVERSITY

WIPF & STOCK · Eugene, Oregon

Wipf and Stock Publishers
199 W 8th Ave, Suite 3
Eugene, OR 97401

Immanuel Kant 1724-1924
Addresses given at Jacob Sleeper Hall, Boston,
on the Two Hundredth Anniversary of Kant's Birth.
By Wilm, E. C.
ISBN 13: 978-1-5326-1896-3
Publication date 10/12/2017
Previously published by Yale University Press, 1925

DUTY

SUBLIME AND MIGHTY NAME, THAT DOST
EMBRACE NOTHING CHARMING OR INSINUAT-
ING, BUT REQUIREST SUBMISSION, WHAT ORIGIN
IS THERE WORTHY OF THEE, AND WHERE IS
THERE TO BE FOUND THE ROOT OF THY NOBLE
DESCENT, WHICH PROUDLY REJECTS ALL
KINDRED WITH THE INCLINATIONS?

KANT

EDITOR'S PREFACE

THE following papers, with the exception of Mr. Shapley's, contain the substance of addresses given at Jacob Sleeper Hall, Boston, on the two-hundredth anniversary of Kant's birth, April 22, 1924. A few alterations and additions have been made here and there in preparing the materials for the press; but the papers remain substantially as delivered. It is hoped that they may be of interest to a wider public.

E. C. WILM.

CONTENTS

INTRODUCTORY

GEORGE HERBERT PALMER

W E are gathered here tonight to rejoice that two centuries ago an Earth-shaker was born, one who made a turning-point in human thought, like Socrates, like Copernicus, like Darwin. Those who deal with philosophy before him seem like men before the flood. No one can write intelligently on philosophy after 1781 without making up his accounts with Kant. On almost every subject of human inquiry he has set his mark. Beginning with Mathematics, Physics, and Astronomy, absorbing much from the English and French Empiricists as well as from dogmatic writers as far apart as Wolff and Rousseau, at length in his three Critiques—*The Pure Reason,* 1781, *The Practical Reason,* 1788, *Judgment,* 1790—he pushed his destructive and transforming path through the deepest problems of nature, man, and God, demonstrating that our minds are no mere recipients of knowledge but equal partners in the production of it.

Our Committee has felt that the best way to bring so comprehensive a thinker before our audience is to split him up and induce certain eminent specialists of our neighborhood to sum up in ten-minute speeches his teaching in their several fields. The width of his appeal thus becomes striking. But the plan has its infelicities. Kant is all made in one piece and cannot be broken up without distortion. We have merely chosen the lesser of two evils. In a couple of hours no single speaker could make the huge bulk of Kant so intelligible as our seven interpreters.

Before examining the work of Kant it is well to have in mind a picture of the man himself, and I have been asked to remind you of the few facts of his life and the traits of his simple but massive character. By circumstance and disposition the quiet scholar whom I have called an Earth-shaker seems peculiarly unfitted for such a rôle. From the beginning of his life in 1724 to its end in 1804 he was encompassed with such restrictions as would have cut off anyone but himself from public notice. These hindering restrictions were of four sorts—local, monetary, bodily, and professional.

East Prussia, the scene of Kant's entire life, lies in the extreme northeast corner of Germany and, being at that time separated from the rest of Prussia by a strip of Poland, it had as close relations with the Russian territory as with Germany. In fact no part of Germany was more remote from cultural influences. Königsberg, Kant's birthplace, was its chief city, with 55,000 inhabitants and a small university. In its Faculty were eight Full and eight Assistant Professors. How many students there were I cannot precisely ascertain; but from indications somewhat later I judge that in Kant's time they did not exceed three hundred and that there were not more than 50,000 volumes in the University Library. Such were the restricted surroundings of Kant's entire life. He never travelled. During the stern years of his work as a private tutor he lived for a while in a country town sixty miles distant from Königsberg. But more than seventy years were spent in the place of his birth, from which he was not absent for a night in forty years. In Königsberg itself he had no house of his own till he was fifty-nine, but was a changing lodger in one unsatisfactory boarding house after another. Such was the local, provincial, person who proved to be a world's man.

But there are more restrictions than those of locality. Kant was poor, not merely a man of small means, but severely, pinchingly, poor. His father earned a meagre support by work on leather straps used in harnesses. But there were eleven children, more than half dying young and half-fed. When the pious parents died there was no money for the fees then exacted for a religious service, and they were buried as paupers. Kant's sisters were domestic servants. After passing through the free public school Kant spent the years 1746-1747 at the University. For nine years following the death of his father in 1746 he supported himself as a private tutor—a kind of upper servant—in three wealthy families. He was therefore thirty-one before he was able even to offer himself for an academic career. In the German universities there is a nondescript sort of teacher, called a Privatdozent, who receives no official pay but, being a scholar of promise who has already attained the Doctor's degree, is licensed to lecture on whatever subjects he will, and to receive fees from any students who care to attend. Such an unsalaried lecturer was Kant from 1755 to 1770. He had entered his forty-seventh year when he obtained a professorship. The long delay was not due to lack of recognition. The number of places was small, and the poverty following Prussia's Seven Years' War obliged reduction, not increase of the staff. Kant's salary as a Professor was $300, which in the last ten years of his life rose to $600.

But he was restricted in health no less than by

poverty, his figure slight, little more than five feet, and his spine somewhat curved—"a man of an incurving chest and a retiring disposition," my predecessor, Professor Bowen, used to call him. Throughout life his health, especially in lungs and stomach, called for constant care. Abstemiousness and regular habits ruled his days. Even after he had a home of his own, he, like most German students, took but one full meal a day, a cup of coffee and a slice of bread serving for breakfast and supper. Rising was invariably at five o'clock, a walk at four, bed at ten. A single servant, Lampe, attended to all his wants; for, of course, he was unmarried. Indeed he may be said to have been born unmarried.

Such restrictions could not fail to leave deep marks on the character of the man himself. Inevitably he became a functionary, exhibiting in exaggerated form the traits of his class, the Professor, the Academic person. Only in two of the great houses where he had served as tutor did Kant ever come in contact with the graces of life, the ease and play of spirit which come where wealth and leisure bring familiarity with the world at large. Nothing like wealth or leisure ever entered this life. Too kind and mentally alert to be in the least boorish, with unobtrusive modest

5

manners, vivacious speech and a shining eye, Kant still always remained a man of the cloister, insatiable of books and measuring the work of existence by the number of working hours its days might dutifully yield. It is true that in writing he seems always engaged in research, in clearing his own mind, rather than in imparting knowledge to another. But this nobler aim only makes his style the more academic and for the common man inaccessible. When the matter under discussion is already familiar to himself he passes it over, however weighty, in a few lines. When he is himself perplexed the reader must find his way unaided through pages of repetition and experiment. Perhaps the two most important books of modern times—the two at least which we could wish to have received most care in publication—are Shakespeare's First Folio and Kant's *Critique of Pure Reason*. Yet on almost every page of the sacred Folio we rightly suspect errors of the press, and the *Critique* extends no helping hand to one wading through its profundities. It was meditated for twelve years, written in five months. In it sentences struggle to inordinate lengths. Technical terms abound, enlarging their meaning as the writer proceeds. Divisions and subdivisions are invented to keep the thing in order, where not formal order but clarity of thought is what is wanted. A worse piece of composition can hardly be found. It embodied all that has ever been urged against German professorial style. And, curiously enough, its world importance is closely connected with these very defects. Kant's reach exceeds his grasp. For his successors he opened many paths whose ends he could not himself discern. Recognizing, however, that we are dealing tonight with a man essentially academic, our Committee has thought that we should approach him most suitably, by appearing in scholar's gowns rather than in conventional evening dress.

At first thought it would seem astounding that a man burdened with such restrictions should have so widely benefited his species that two hundred years later companies should quite naturally gather to do him honor. How has it happened? What compensatory advantage did he possess which we have hitherto overlooked? There was none. Kant merely turned his quadruple limitations inside out, transmuting them to powers. Bacon tells us that nature is conquered by obeying her, a saying as applicable to human nature as to physical. A man of sense wastes no time lamenting adverse circumstances. Cheerfully accepting their guidance and turning his back on despondency, he studies how by insight, resourcefulness, patience, and persistent will he may draw from the circumstances in which he finds himself assistance for his plans. Kant did so. Let us come close to him and more justly estimate the four doubtful features of his career.

His childhood was certainly fortunate. Poor as his parents were, they brought him a rich endowment. He tells us how he acquired his idea of fairmindedness. The saddlers of Königsberg, a superior trade, tried to crush out strap-making on which the Kant family depended for support. Kant says that through all the controversy no harsh word came from his father, who often pointed out how naturally such an issue might arise. Kant's mother left him permanently grateful for the beauty she showed him in the fields and in poetry. Both parents were profoundly religious. That was the family tradition, and in Kant's youth a wave of Pietism swept through the land. Its leader in Königsberg was a remarkable man, Schultz, an intimate of the Kant household and both Professor in the University and Director of the excellent high school where Kant learned to love Latin. It was Schultz who advised Kant to enter the University after his mother's death. German Pietism, like our own Puritanism, laid its chief stress on the responsibility of the individual soul to God. It cared little for churches and ceremonial, but every hour heard a divine voice summoning to some duty which might ally the obedient man more closely with God. What better inspiration could be had for the arduously monotonous life to be led by Kant than the conviction bred in boyhood that freedom could everywhere be had by obedience to a law, not alien indeed to his own good, but hourly necessary for any serviceable connection with the outside world? Take away from Kant the categorical imperative, and he would be a Samson with shorn hair. Most of us submit to duty when we cannot avoid it. Kant joyfully leaned on it, was supported by it, and saw hardship disappear at its touch. And what spot more favorable for acquiring this tremendous engine of success than a quiet town where human interests might be deep but could not well be various? We cannot call conditions bad or good in themselves. Their quality springs from the man who meets them. Those of Königsberg, unfavorable as they might be for most of us, were fortunate for the stout heart of Kant.

Kant's poverty was severe and continuous, but we must not exaggerate either its degree or importance. Most German students are poor. They seem to take it undisturbed and pretty much as a matter of course. I often used to wonder at the small sums on which friends of mine jauntily kept life going. Kant had an advantage over most in that he lived at home during school and university years. An uncle too, a shoemaker, helped him with small sums—I cannot learn how large—during his university course. For nine years after the death of his father in 1746 he lived in three other homes. Even during the dreary fifteen years of his unsalaried lectureship he was not penniless. In 1760 a small librarianship was given him, which yielded fifty dollars a year; and it must be remembered that money was then worth at least five times what it is today. His main support, however, came from student fees. These are often more considerable than the official salary. How large they were in his case is not recorded. But to win them he must make his courses attractive and as varied in subject as possible. It is said that his teaching was animated, full of humor, narrative, and exact knowledge. To a man of interests so wide the call to deal with a mass of miscellaneous information was not obnoxious; it took much of the place of travel and society, while enabling him to maintain himself till preferment came. But, after all, what helped Kant most to meet the long delay was the

habit he had gained of getting twenty-six cents'
worth out of every quarter, and spending fewer
quarters than other men. In a stripped life he
could be content. Yet with all this careful living
Kant was generous. He entertained, always after
he had a home of his own having several guests
at dinner; he looked after those poorer than himself, helping his brothers and sisters, and saving a
substantial sum to protect after his death those
who had been dependent on him in life.

Feeble health is no advantage to anyone, though
sooner or later it comes to most of us. Those who
up to middle life have never known a pain are the
ones to be pitied. When the inevitable break falls
on them, it is apt to be disastrous. Such persons
have had no practice in the proper care of health,
and if so late they attempt it, they are likely
enough to color their watchfulness with mor-
bidity. Those whose early years were feeble often
outlive the strong. Knowing that sound bodies are
rare and that much of the hard work of the world
has been done by semi-invalids, they are ready to
take their infirmities soberly and gradually to dis-
cover how to dispose of them in their system with
the least harm. Such was the understanding of
Kant. In spite of a slender frame, his enormous
work was never checked by weakness till his very

last years; and dying at eighty he had an advantage over most of his contemporaries.

But the question remains: Was what Kant gained worth what he paid for it? Grant that he was a great professor and a large benefactor, too, of the world that came after him, yet who of us would accept a life so stern and bare, so stripped of graces and wonderments, so humdrum as to border on the comic? Of course not! No one would take that life for his own, and just because it was made to fit Kant. We must beware of setting up a standard pattern of man and assuming that anyone departing from it is of an inferior order. The very opposite is the case. Standard men are made of common stuff. Great ones follow patterns of their own. We enlarge our conceptions of mankind by studying them closely. But we must bear in mind that to reach any high excellence we are obliged to accept limitations. Excellences are not altogether compatible. A pretty good chemist may be a pretty good musician, but he will not be a master in either field. The persistent specialist is usually somewhat maimed and one-sided, and will not be much disturbed if he excites amusement in those who prefer completeness to depth. Kant's manhood contained nothing but what he had dreamed of as a boy. He followed the single course permitted by his restrictions. But he poured into its narrow bounds love and enthusiasm, and transformed its restrictions amazingly. His studies took him over the entire universe, from the starry heavens above to the moral law within. He was no narrow pedant. Paulsen enumerates thirteen subjects of his lecture courses, favorites among them being Anthropology, Physical Geography, and Teaching. Books of travel and foreign politics interested him intensely. Every stage of the American and French Revolutions he watched sympathetically, being himself a Republican. To novels and poetry he was not averse, was on kindly terms with his townspeople, beloved by his students, and a voluminous correspondent. His books and pamphlets I will not venture to count. Welcome, if deferred, was the praise they brought. Each day close contact with friends was secured by having two or three at dinner. This lasted from one till four, a feast of talk rather than of food. Here everything but Philosophy was discussed. Philosophy was banished and so relief was gained for him whose chief concern it was the rest of the day. A rich and happy life! Thrilling in its subjugation of circumstance, in its daily good cheer, its volume and originality of production. To most of us its ordered regularity is repellent, if not in-

conceivable. As I wonderingly survey it, a stanza
of George Herbert comes to my mind:

> Slight those who say amidst their sickly healths
>   Thou liv'st by rule. What doth not so but man?
> Houses are built by rule, and commonwealths.
>   Entice the trusty sun, if that thou can,
> From his ecliptick line. Beckon the sky.
> Who lives by rule then keeps good company.

This exalted companionship Kant had all through
his disciplined years, and it made the poor and
consumptive little figure from narrow Königsberg a moral and intellectual hero.

Of his influence since his death little need be
said. It is too well known. Jowett of Balliol used
to be given the praise of a great teacher, that his
many pupils differed widely from him and from
one another. Thus it was with Kant. Fichte,
Schelling, Hegel, Schopenhauer were his eldest
children, but children with minds of their own.
In England his thought affected men as widely
apart as Coleridge, Carlyle, Mansel, Maurice,
and Caird. To America it came in still more at-
tenuated form as Concord Transcendentalism. Indeed the majority of us are probably different
from what we should be had Kant not been born,
so pervasive has his influence been even over those

who never heard his name. I owe him a deep personal debt. After struggling for many years with the arbitrary limitations of English Empiricism, I found in him my liberator. I never became a Kantian. Few are that. But I gained an idealistic method, I learned the primacy of the Practical Reason, and I acquired a lifelong admiration for the man "who broke the bands of circumstance and grappled with his evil star."

KNOWLEDGE

MARY WHITON CALKINS

NO loyal student will hesitate, however keen
his sense of disability, to speak in honor of
a master. So I who owe much to Immanuel Kant
have not ventured to refuse the invitation to ad-
dress you briefly on his doctrine of knowledge,
though I know that what I shall say must be over-
familiar.

I shall not, I trust, seem to give the lie to what
I have just said of my debt to Kant if I next con-
fess to the deep resentments which I hold against
him. I resent, in the first place, the outer form of
the *Critique of Pure Reason:* the barbarism of its
style; its use at once high-handed and inconsistent
of conventional terms in new senses; and, most of
all, its exasperating habit of stringing out, under
strange headings and in misleading guise of
novelty, repetitions of the same discussion.[1] And
even keener than my objections to the form are my
criticisms of the metaphysical shortcomings, as I
deem them, of the great *Critique.* Some of these

[1] *Cf.* E. Adickes, edition of Kant's *Kritik der reinen
Vernunft,* pp. XXI ff., XXIV; footnotes of pp. 139 ff.

17

will disclose themselves in the course of my brief exposition of Kant's teaching; but on one of them I shall lay stress at the outset, my objection to that distinction between appearance and reality which forms so prominent a part of the *Critique* that a recent commentator, Norman Kemp Smith, treats it as the pivotal problem of the book.[2] Yet this conception of reality, which stands opposed to fact or phenomenon, constitutes a needless obstruction to Kant's essential argument.

I have so ungraciously begun with criticism that you may not regard me as a Kantian *per fas et nefas*, a blind and uncritical follower. My respect for Kant triumphs over my sense of the needless perplexities, the essential inconsistencies, and the significant shortcomings of his philosophy. For in spite of his reactionary doctrines, he made an incomparable gift to philosophy by deflecting eighteenth-century epistemology from no fewer than three mischievous channels. To drop my metaphor: the *Critique of Pure Reason* (1) in the first place, by its wholesome insistence on the sense-factor in knowledge, effectively counteracted the superb disregard and disdain of sense which marked the Wolffian distortion of Leibniz' teach-

[2] *A Commentary to Kant's Critique of Pure Reason,* 1918, pp. 270-280 ff. and *passim.*

ing. (2) In the second place, by his category-doctrine Kant quite as effectively corrected the one-sided sensationalism of Hume's impression-doctrine. The experienced object, he teaches, is indeed a complex of sensations spatially and temporally ordered, but it is also a unified, serially ordered and causally related object; and all these relations as truly belong to it, as truly are a part of it, as its color or its shape. This truth, later so significantly if tortuously developed by Hegel, Kant was first to teach. And we must not lose sight of the importance of the doctrine by the obscurities with which Kant himself invests it—by the artificial cleavage which he makes between sense and thought, and by the quite gratuitous problem, which he raises, of the method of applying categories to sensations.

Last (3) and in my view of crowning importance is Kant's doctrine that essential to knowledge is the knower and that implicit in our knowledge of the object is our experience of this knower. Basal to the category of unity, he teaches, is the unifying knower; essential to recognition, the awareness of present object as identical with past object, is the continuing, the identifying, self. "I am conscious of myself as identical," he says, even "in the various determinations presented to me in perception." It is true, of course, that in the Paralogisms Kant virtually loses hold upon this doctrine by the ill-considered teaching that the self is unknown; and it is also true that his recapture of the self, conceived as free moral being, never puts him squarely back in his old secure position. None the less Kant's doctrine of knowledge, as centered in both editions in the *Analytik,* is unmistakably a conception of the knowing self.

The ears of contemporary philosophers grow deafer and deafer to the arguments of Kant. Yet I permit myself the observation that there are things undreamt of in much present-day philosophy to which, if we would but listen to him, the little Königsberg professor might "put us wise." Let me run back over the factors which I have stressed in his system of knowledge.

There is, first, his stress on the sense-factor in knowledge; and here I hasten to admit that this generation needs neither Kant, nor any other metaphysical "Daniel come to judgment," to persuade it of the important rôle of sensation in knowledge. Kant, of course, means by 'sense' to indicate the affective and impulsive as well as the sensational side of experience; and perhaps the most widespread of the tendencies of modern psychology and experience-theory is its stress upon the instinctive urges and dynamic impulses as both primitive and central in experience.

It follows that the second of Kant's characteristic doctrines about knowledge is nowadays in ill repute. For in our interest in the instinctive springs of experience, fortified by our wholly justified reaction against undiluted rationalism, with its over-abstractions, we have quite lost out of sight the experienced fact of relating; in our insistence that sense and impulse constitute one factor of knowledge we have quite ignored the other factor, thinking.

The third and last of the constituent conceptions of Kant's epistemology is that described in his preposterous jargon as the doctrine of the transcendental unity of apperception—in plain words, the doctrine that a knowledge of objects is impossible without a self which knows. Here, assuredly, is a doctrine which is challenged from every side. Ingenious realists seek to undermine it by urging that precisely because we can never get rid of the self we ought, epistemologically, to ignore it. And, more concretely, the behaviorists —rejecting with Kant the Humian fiction of abstract "states of consciousness"—unceremoniously oust the self to make room for the 'whole organism,' the body, in its reaction to the environment. And yet there are those of us who still believe that neither realist nor behaviorist rightly reads experience; that the ubiquitous self cannot be banished; that bodily reactions accompany or condition but do not constitute knowledge; finally, that knowledge is the function of a knower.

ETHICS

E. C. WILM

I

IT is particularly appropriate for us here in New England and in America to celebrate this anniversary, since the first of American thinkers, Ralph Waldo Emerson, a native of New England and of Boston, owes the most distinctive feature of his own thinking directly to Kant. Emerson has himself recorded this debt in a notable passage in his lecture, The Transcendentalist, delivered in Boston in 1842, a passage which is of interest here not only because it indicates clearly Emerson's own philosophical affiliations, but because it states, with extraordinary lucidity and strength, the central position of the Kantian philosophy. "It is well known to most of my audience," he writes, "that the Idealism of the present day acquired the name of Transcendental from the use of that term by Immanuel Kant, of Königsberg, who replied to the skeptical philosophy of Locke, which insisted that there was nothing in the intellect which was not previously in the experience of the senses, by showing that there was a very important class of ideas, or imperative forms, which did not come by experience, but through which experience was acquired; that these were intuitions of the mind itself; and he denominated them transcendental forms. The extraordinary profoundness and precision of that man's thinking have given vogue to his nomenclature, in Europe and America, to that extent, that whatever belongs to the class of intuitive thought, is popularly called at the present day Transcendental."

It is a useful aid to the understanding of Kant's ethics to remember that Kant's philosophy, in spite of certain incoherences, is integral, and that the same presuppositions and points of view which are discernible in his metaphysics dominate his ethics throughout. From the fact that the substructure of Kant's theory of knowledge and of his metaphysics was laid down first in the *Inaugural Dissertation* and in the first *Critique,* it is natural to suppose that the theory of knowledge, with the doctrine of the forms of intuition, was primary in Kant's thinking, and that the ethical theories were elaborated in conformity with the results reached in the theory of knowledge. But the events of a man's interior history do not al-

ways follow the same sequences as the happenings
of his public life; and if the evolution of Kant's
spiritual history were as well known as the dates
of his writings, it would not be surprising to find
that the priority lay elsewhere than supposed.
"Was für eine Philosophie man hat," Fichte once
said, "kommt darauf an was für ein Mensch man
ist:" the kind of philosophy you hold depends
upon the kind of man you are. And an intimate
knowledge of the interrelations of Kant's person-
ality and his work would, I imagine, reveal the
fact that Kant's idealistic metaphysics rests upon
the moral idealism of his ethical convictions, and
these, in turn, upon the conscientious austerities,
the moral ambitiousness of an honorable, uncom-
promising, and somewhat self-assertive person-
ality, whose sharply stamped traits were by no
means softened, but accentuated, rather, by the pie-
tistic influences of his parentage and youthful
training. A fit temperament, this, for his northern,
seagirt home, where only men of tougher fibre can
make good their will against nature's rude, irra-
tional forces. To live constantly in their presence is
likely to engender in men in whom susceptibility
and nobleness of nature are finely mingled a certain pessimism, particularly if the conflicts without
are matched by conflicts within. This mood is elo-

quently expressed in Romain Rolland's *Jean-Christophe,* in a passage which reminds vividly of the Kantian ethics. "He saw that life is a battle without armistice, without mercy, in which he who wishes to be worthy of the name of a man must forever fight against whole armies of invisible enemies; against the murderous forces of nature, uneasy desires, dark thoughts, treacherously leading him to degradation and destruction. . . . He saw that happiness and love were only the friends of a moment to lead the heart to disarm and abdicate. . . . And the little puritan heard the voice of God: Go on to suffer, you who must suffer. You do not live to be happy. You live to fulfil my law."

To the student of Kant's works themselves, in any event, the resemblance between his position in metaphysics and ethics is noteworthy. In both spheres (like Plato), he seeks to vindicate the place of reason in contrast to desire, of the supra-sensible in contrast to the life of sense. In the age-old conflict between rationalism and empiricism, he champions the former against the latter, although he is wary enough (especially in his theory of knowledge) to guard against the extravagances of the older rationalism, from which, in his view, philosophy has unduly suffered. And so, as everyone knows, he took up a midway position, magnifying, in a way hitherto unknown, the place and function of reason, while not neglecting the indispensable rôle of sense perception, in the structure of experience as a whole. We turn to a brief exposition of his general conceptions, with a hope of gaining a view, not too crude and too alien to Kant's own thought, as it actually took shape in his mind.

II

Kant's attention was early drawn to the extraordinary difference between two kinds of knowledge, one which depends wholly upon observation, and another which seems to exist *a priori*, independently of any empirical basis. So the knowledge of the shape of the earth, or of the distances of the various planets from the sun, or, say, of the peculiar markings of some species of animal,—such knowledge is not gained by intuition, nor can it be obtained by any process of abstract reasoning about the nature of the objects dealt with. Our knowledge here comes entirely from observation, is empirical. It is quite otherwise with another kind of knowledge, which seems to arise without the preliminary empirical investigation of particular instances. Thus the geometrical properties of a triangle can be determined without an actual observation of triangles, by thought; and what is found to be true of one triangle, will be known to be true of all. So also we know, according to Kant, that every effect has a cause, and every cause an effect, and that this relation is universal throughout nature, in spite of the fact that our actual acquaintance with nature is finite and circumscribed. Our knowledge is universal, but experience is always particular.

The reason for the remarkable difference is, in Kant's view, that in geometrical objects, and in your thought about causal relations, you are not dealing with the crude materials of sensation, which can, of course, be apprehended only by sense perception, but with relations among them, of space, time, degree, causation, and the like, and that these relations have no objective existence, but are the creatures of intelligence. Relations are not objects of sense perception but have a merely mental existence. They are not objects of knowledge, Kant is fond of saying, but conditions of knowledge, indispensable forms or moulds, types of organization, without which knowledge, in any proper sense, could never come to exist. In this way a certain stability and order, enough to make science possible, is conferred upon an otherwise chaotic and shifting sense-manifold, a mere heap of isolated particulars, devoid of coherence or of any rational significance.

The posture of affairs in the realm of morality is not dissimilar. The raw materials here are men's desires and wishes, the cravings of sense. But these, like the sense impressions which enter into knowledge, are devoid of any principle of order, and hence incapable, in themselves, of con-stituting a moral universe. Nor will the mind gain any real knowledge with which to guide conduct through any empirical search. In your quest for knowledge here, as in the realm of nature, you have two possibilities before you. You can hope to determine the moral quality of an act by an em-pirical test, by asking about its consequences, its conduciveness to some empirically identifiable good, some utility, or happiness, or some other ob-ject which the act tends to realize. In metaphysics, as we saw, the empirical method failed to give uni-versality and necessity, and valid science. Here it is no better. The moral laws which would result from such an empirical investigation would be merely contingent and temporary, calling for only such acts as fulfilled the passing caprice. Such laws would have the doubtful form, "Do this if you would obtain that." But the moral law is not thus contingent, requiring only a conditional obedience. It is categorical; its mandate is simple and unambiguous. It says: "Do this." Obviously, such a law can never be derived from the material of sensuous desire, any more than the form of space can be derived from the sense-material of external nature. The promptings of sense and the demands of the moral law stand in irreconcilable contradiction.

It is now seen what is meant by the primacy, in Kant, of reason and will. In the moral life, as in nature, the reason is legislative and mandatory. "Nothing in the whole world, or even outside of the world," Kant says in the opening sentence of *The Metaphysic of Morality,* "can possibly be regarded as good without limitation except a good will." But what is the good will? What does the good will demand? Kant gives the answer in an equally famous passage in the same work: "As the will must not be moved to act from any desire for the results to follow from obedience to a certain law, the only principle of will which remains is that of the conformity of actions to universal law. In all cases I must act in such a way *that I can at the same time will that my maxim should become a universal law.* This is what is meant by conformity to law pure and simple; and this is the principle which serves, and must serve, to determine the will, if the idea of duty is not to be regarded as empty and chimerical."

Kant illustrates his position by several kinds of action which, by the test he proposes, are seen to be clearly evil. Promise-breaking, for example, is a kind of action whose principle cannot be universalized, since, if everyone broke his promises, promise-breaking would become impossible. So with theft or suicide. The principles of both are self-contradictory. Universalized, such actions would destroy themselves. There can be no stealing without property; the principle of this act contains a self-contradiction, and is not workable. Thus, as Dewey says, "looked at in the light of reason every mean, insincere, inconsiderate motive of action shrivels into a private exception which a person wants to take advantage of in his own favor, and which he would be horrified to have others act upon. It violates the great principle of logic that A is A. Kindly, decent acts, on the contrary, extend and multiply themselves in a continuing harmony."[1]

It will serve to bring out a little further the rigidity of the Kantian morality if I set down together a few other characteristic points in his ex-

[1] *Human Nature and Conduct,* 1922, p. 246.

position. (1) An act has no moral value if it is for any reason necessitated; it is then a mere product of nature, not of the moral will; (2) it has no merit if it merely conforms to some externally imposed law; nor even (3) if it conforms to the central moral principle of consistency, if the motive for the act is anything else than respect for the law itself; nor (4) if it proceeds from inclination or a sensuous motive of any kind. An inclination to duty is indeed impossible, since the sensuous man can act only from egoistic motives, to which the law, through its very nature, opposes itself.

It is evident that the break between the sensuous and the supersensuous worlds is complete. Seldom in modern literature has the conflict between the "flesh" and the "spirit" found a more effective expression than in Kant's sombre deliberations. It is the same conflict which has been depicted with solemn grandeur by the literature and art of the ages. Two ways open before every man: the path of pleasure, on the one side; on the other, the *via dolorosa*. Before this stern alternative, morality leaves no choice but renunciation. "Sense is the nail," Plato says with incomparable grandeur (the passage is in the *Phædo*), "by which the soul is fastened to the body, and the soul can be liberated and return to its source only after the oblivion and death of the passions." To this view Kant unconditionally subscribes, and he gives to it a more weighty argumentative support than any other writer in the history of philosophy.

III

We may close our brief sketch by indicating a few criticisms, without attempting to elucidate them at length. (1) The principle of consistency, so central in Kant's system, does not hold in all cases. Some acts, like deeds of charity, are good, but only as exceptions. The principle of charity cannot be universalized; for, in the first place, only those who have can give, and, secondly, if all of this class were charitable, there would be no further use for charity; indeed, charity would be impossible; if persisted in, it would, like the evil acts cited above, destroy itself. (2) The consistency principle really implies a good, which Kant formally denies; so the real objection to stealing is evidently not that stealing destroys itself, but that it destroys something deemed valuable, in this case, the institution of property; the same is true of promise-breaking, homicide, and the rest. Thus our knowledge of moral laws is not an intuition, but is the result of reflection upon the potential results of acts. (3) Happiness, which Kant disparages as an end of action, is included by Kant in his definition of the supreme good, and he even held that, unless virtue and happiness are ultimately united, the universe ceases to be rational. Thus a good, which is denied any legitimate place in ethics, is implied in Kant's whole moral theology. Finally, (4) the common sense of mankind has repudiated the harsh asceticism of Kant's ethics, which denied to feeling any place in the moral life. Indeed, it may be said that with the evolution of moral character, the harsh opposition between law and sense, of which Kant made so much, tends to disappear, love annulling both law and fear. In the higher regions of morality, as the poet Schiller eloquently urged, the sharp contrast between inclination and duty, law and freedom, becomes more and more obscured. Not inclination and duty, but inclination to duty, is the ideal constitution of man. Thus grace and beauty of conduct supplant the stern austerity of the life of reluctant obedience to duty. Everyone has known those characters from whose life every trace of discord and obstruction has been removed, for whom duty has become a pleasant task. Such characters are indeed the ripest fruit, as Emerson thought, of moral discipline. "When we see a soul whose acts are regal, graceful, and pleasant as roses, we must thank God that such things can be and are, and not turn sourly on the angel and say, Crump is the better man, with his grunting resistance to all his native devils."

Great merits remain. It was Kant's permanent service to have connected deeply the idea of autonomy with morality, no act being entitled to the rank of a moral act which does not flow from the free agency of man, or which aims at any mere compliance or outward conformity. Secondly, he grasped the very essence of morality in his subordination of the part to the whole, the isolated desire to the interest and meaning of life as a whole, —which is the real significance, I take it, of his principle of universality, and of his emphasis on the great concepts of duty and law. Through his rugged championship of reason against desire and caprice, he exerted a wholesome influence upon the shallow, eudæmonistic moral philosophy of his own time, and he has wielded an incalculable influence over the moral reflection and the practical conduct of mankind since his day.

That he did not create a flawless and final system was, of course, inevitable, and is perhaps not to be regretted. "The best part of truth," says

Emerson in a brilliant sentence of his *Journals,* "is certainly that which hovers in gleams and suggestions, unpossessed, before man. His recorded knowledge is dead and cold. But this chorus of thoughts and hopes, these dawning truths, like great stars just lifting themselves into his horizon, they are his future, and console him for the ridiculous brevity and meanness of his civic life."

THE POSTULATES

WILLIAM ERNEST HOCKING

S YSTEMS of thought, like mountain ranges, are subject to an erosion which leaves their mightiest rocks salient. In any view of Kant's thought, after two hundred years, his three postulates regarding human freedom, immortality, and God, must stand out like gaunt peaks, barren of verdure, but firm as the everlasting foundations, and at home with the sunset and the sunrise.

Like so much else in Kant's thought, they invite a certain confidence by their very bleakness, and the force of the negations from which they arise. For these negations are latent in almost every mind. Some men are ready to affirm God and the survival of death with unshaken certainty; and some others as roundly deny them. But most men do both,—sometimes reaching a momentary assurance in their favor: "It must be so, that there is a God in the world"; and sometimes an equal assurance of denial: "It cannot be so." For after all, every analogy of nature is against them.

Kant's greatness consists largely in the steady acuteness with which he feels both this No and

37

this Yes, and undertakes to do justice to both. As a natural scientist, a student of Newton, an original explorer of the stellar universe, proposer of a nebular hypothesis, he finds no God in the world of physical law, no room there for freedom, no sign of immortality. He is ready to defend the principles of a rigorously mathematical natural science against all comers. He will have no compromise with superstition: he can allow his imagination no standing room in a supernatural world in which no propositions can be tested, no objects discerned and related to objects we otherwise know,—in which, therefore, all would-be seers are really ghost-seers, and are at liberty to see what ghosts they will. Kant is an unsparing destroyer of illusion.

But he also perceives that the rational interest in what is beyond nature can never be simply snubbed and cut off without satisfaction. A lesser agnostic would be satisfied to point out the law of relativity which makes it impossible for the eagle of knowledge to outsoar the atmosphere of natural experience: but Kant's attention is held by the fact that it persists in trying to do so. If we say, We can know nothing but phenomena, we let out the secret that there are Noumena to be reckoned with. We cannot exclude science from the world of reality without knowing that we are doing so, and therefore touching the edge of that world in the process of denying ourselves entrance. It is impossible to draw up a complete renunciation of our metaphysical claim.

So when the human mind struggles with the contradictory propositions: God exists, God does not exist, Kant makes no haste to close the issue by saying (as the first *Critique* would seem to require) that both propositions deal with the inconceivable, and are therefore devoid of meaning. He says, instead, "The human understanding cannot decide for nor against; reason is in equilibrium;" and in saying this, he admits that, in spite of the absence of a God-object in the world, some sort of meaning the idea of God still has, and the question of God's being is not nonsense!

For cognitive meanings are not the only meanings. There are also the meanings a sign may have for action. The flash of the lighthouse light is less an optical image than a direction to the pilot's arm. The sound of the alarm-clock bell is less a series of musical tones than a summons to the sleepy will. Cognitive meanings tend to vanish into their active correlates as habit quickens the interpretation. The engineer hardly sees the brakeman's signal,—he performs it: the musician hardly sees the printed notes,—he executes their meaning. In these cases, the vision remains a necessary condition of the action: if darkness obscures the notes, the musician can no longer play them. But this evanescence of cognitive meaning suggests the question whether there may not be some ideas wholly devoid of sensuous objectivity which may still have a full and definite import for action. Perhaps metaphysical ideas are of this sort. Everyone will agree that the pictorial imagery which surrounds the propositions of the creed is devoid of verisimilitude to any discoverable objects. It is like the mediæval portraits of Christ or Mary, projection of an inner feeling and fantasy. Religion has commonly made as much of the cognitive contents of its creeds as of their practical applications; but the common judgment of men has placed the essence of religion in the latter,—in the reinforcement it gives to the 'higher' (and impulsively weaker) motives of action. The meaning of the creed tends to reduce to its moral bearing. And occasionally the suggestion appears that this practical purport is the essence of the religious idea: so that he "that wills to do the will of my Father" already has the clue to the meaning of doctrine.

These suggestions in common consciousness Kant brings to full and explicit affirmation. In matters of metaphysics, the practical reason has something to say for itself where theoretical reason is in abeyance. The practical reason has the 'primacy.' It gives laws to the theoretical reason as the theoretical reason gives laws to nature. It can certainly not oppose any evidence of the understanding. Nor can it fill a region, left unoccupied by the understanding, with arbitrary pleasing fancies: because one likes the paradise of Mahomet, one has no license to believe it. But the practical reason may oppose itself to a certain reluctance of the theoretical reason to allow that empty region to be occupied at all: a dog-in-the-manger attitude which takes the form of an appeal for indefinite suspense of judgment. If the practical reason has certain necessary interests which carry speculative positions with them by equal necessity, then theoretical reason cannot refuse to allow these positions to be taken. The necessities of the moral will may become, not the choices but the necessities, of belief.

But how does it happen that the practical reason touches this *terra incognita* at all? It is because, at one point, it has dealings with a level of reality deeper than that which the intellect can reach. That point is the consciousness of duty. For the whole distinction of duty is that it calls upon us to take charge of the self of experience and rule it. Everything in us that belongs simply to 'nature,' the self of desires, passions, instincts, and complexes, the self of which psychology and anthropology apprise us, is subject to causal law. But man is the being that *makes psychology,*—a fact which psychology sometimes overlooks,—and when he thus describes his own factors, he knows that he is more than the things described. In the act of knowing his own 'nature,' he puts that nature down as a *part* of himself, not the whole of it; though as a theorist he cannot remain satisfied with less than the whole of available truth. It is only in his moral self that he resolves the paradox; for as a moral agent, he knows that his 'nature' is to be made subject to the moral law.

Grant Kant this conviction which he shares with the common consciousness of mankind, that the sense of duty lies deeper in reality than the psychological self, and the universe opens its infinities, through the "postulates," as the physical cosmos through the "starry heavens above us." It will not be amiss, on this occasion, to retrace the familiar argument of these deservedly noted passages.

_____

First of all, the 'ought' is meaningless unless it is possible to fulfil it. If I am under obligation, I must be free: but "I ought; and therefore, I can." This freedom cannot become an item of theoretical knowledge. It remains a postulate, *i.e.,* something I am bound to affirm as I accept the demand of duty.

But having taken this step, I must take another. The moral law is not satisfied by my doing this and that duty, as questions of duty arise. It requires that I shall *want* to do what I *ought* to do. Now as we human beings are constituted, duty sets itself in the path of our desires with a thoroughly independent set of requirements: I am chiefly conscious of duty as something I don't altogether want to do. My whole duty, however, is not done until I get beyond this sense of dutifulness. And this means nothing less than that I am called upon to be perfect in my will, which is more than I shall accomplish in any finite time. Does duty, then, demand the impossible? Or is it rather the case that, speaking with the authority of a principle inherently superior to nature, it furnishes a clue to an unsuspected possibility? Assume that the world which touches me with the finger of moral obligation is also a world which makes it possible to fulfil that obligation completely: it must then be a world in which the time necessary for my becoming a perfect, or holy, will is available to me. There must be a continuation of my personal existence beyond the limits which experience presents. Immortality becomes a postulate of the moral will.

Another step is necessary. Personal happiness is something which the dutiful will must make secondary to the 'ought.' But happiness cannot be treated as if it were wholly meaningless, even to the moral will. For when we have an influence over the fortunes of others, as parents over children, or rulers over citizens, we have a natural disposition to assign happiness in accordance with what we call 'desert.' This is what our human sense of justice demands. A moral ruler must be affected by this sense of desert. Now human experience shows very little correspondence between the righteousness of men and their good fortunes. And if what is true of human experience were true throughout the universe, we should have to say that happiness and duty were simply left in a casual independence of each other, sometimes agreeing and sometimes falling apart. And quite apart from one's own lot in the world, one would look on such a condition as a moral chaos; *i.e.,* the world would be as if indifferent to the moral law, as if it had no moral rulership. It would not deserve the name of a just universe: and a doubt of the cosmical validity of the moral law would creep in,—the nerve of duty would be cut. Per contra, if the impulse of duty is to retain its force, the world as a whole must be regarded as a just world: there must be a power which brings about that union of felicity with righteousness which, in his own case, the moral individual can neither obtain nor look to. This power is what mankind has always meant by God. Hence the existence of God is a third postulate of the moral will.

Through the moral law, then, and without enlarging our speculative knowledge at all, we find ourselves members of an order, at once responsible and free, eternal in duration, and divine in destiny.

_____

A few remarks about the position thus reached, in its historical bearings.

The doctrine of the primacy of the will, or practical reason, came to the nineteenth century, deeply affected by the doubts of the metaphysical power of human reason, as a welcome sanction for belief of a positive nature. It could combine readily with agnosticism, because it was agnostic. It created the essentially agnostic system of Fichte. It entered as a factor into Schopenhauer's irrationalism; although Schopenhauer, like Schelling and Bergson, found another alternative in metaphysics: what the intellect cannot reach, that intuition (not will) can discern. It has inspired a type of theology which founds itself upon judgments of value, rather than on judgments of objective truth. And it has evidently something in common with the pragmatic movement of today.

But there are certain important differences between Kant's position and that of pragmatism. In the "will to believe" we have the picture of a launch of faith which may lead to certain definite empirical knowledge. The surgeon who does not know in advance whether his operation will save his patient cannot remain in indefinite suspense of judgment: his will must enter to bring about his decision; and, willing to believe, he then learns whether his belief was justified. Kant's postulates bring no such increase of empirical knowledge.

But this is only one type of pragmatism, and the least systematic type. There is a type of pragmatism according to which the justification of a belief does not lie in a cognitive verification, but in a verification in terms of values. A belief is justified if it bring about a successful adjustment to the world; nay, it is *true* if it so truly guides action. And the success of its guidance may be measured in terms of any positive good, comfort, stimulus, peace, etc. Other pragmatists would limit the good which can verify a belief to the social welfare over long periods of time. But in any case, some type of empirical benefit gives the test of truth.

Kant's position is quite different. It is no empirical good whatever that leads us to adopt a theory. There are no effects of the belief by which it can be tested except the continuing force of the law of duty: and the beliefs in question are germane to the very sphere from which the law of duty emerges. The postulates are not adopted by an act of preference. One does not believe in them because they are felt to be, or found to be, useful to mankind. One does not so much as believe them because it is a duty to do so. One believes them only because one *must,* since the demand of duty cannot be shaken off.

Kant's austerity here deserves to be celebrated. He gives the will no *carte blanche* to establish doctrines for the understanding. And so far as the ethical imperative carries doctrine with it, that doctrine remains theoretically empty of objects, and therefore noninterfering in the work of thought. Religion lives in its moral bearings; it contains not even a premonition of another world, but only an admonition. The metaphysics of the Postulates may thus be regarded as a *metaphysical minimum*.

And just because it is a minimum, it may furnish a refuge to minds caught between affirmation and negation, and yet unable to accept the mental bribe of pragmatism. One may deny all that Kant denies, and remain as austere as Kant remains, and yet have a positive faith which makes the acceptance of duty the rightful bearing of a rational being in the cosmos.

The metaphysical minimum is certainly not enough. It was not enough for Kant himself. I am not referring to certain inner inconsistencies in his argument which might be pointed out. I am referring to the fact that Kant began to find, as he worked his way to the third great *Critique,* an empirical basis for the idea of a purpose in the world. The phrase "practical reason" is an awkward one, confessing a haunting suspicion on Kant's part that, after all, the will that could dictate to theoretical consciousness is a cognitive function. And the true primacy of this function is not to be found in simply moving into unoccupied spaces in the world of possible theory (if there are any such spaces); but rather in placing the contents of causal theory in a more adequate setting. Leibniz had already indicated how this might be done, in his proposition that the causal laws themselves require a teleological explanation.

In the *Critique of Judgment,* Kant is occupied not with the causal order as a whole, but with fragments of nature which call out from us the attributions of value. The great canvas is left unfinished; and the labors of Schopenhauer, Lotze, Royce, still fall within the frame. But the immortality of Kant is as well founded in what he foreshadowed as in what he established for all future time.

SCIENCE

HARLOW SHAPLEY

B EFORE he degenerated into the major philosopher of this minor planet, Immanuel
Kant was a scientist.[1] Before he began his speculations concerning speculation, he speculated
adroitly concerning physical fact. His great subjective analyses were set afloat long after he had
launched a treatise on cosmogony that was, I believe, the finest objective synthesis of science up
to that time. The cosmogony promptly sank. It has
scarcely been heard of since among busy scientists,
except fragmentarily through the occasional yarn
of some reminiscent diver into dark and deep
places.

The *Critiques of Reason*, pure and impure,
have also become so heavily waterlogged that it
takes the special attention of this two hundredth
anniversary of Kant's birth to remind us how

[1] Kant was throughout his life a conscientious student of
science. He lectured and wrote, in addition to the usual
philosophical subjects, on anthropology, physical geography,
theoretical physics, mathematics, mechanics, and mineralogy.
ED.

prettily they rode the German seas for generations on end. The *Critiques,* it is maintained, marked a new era in thought. They analyzed the theory of knowledge, showed the limits of human thinking, established cosmic theism. They were the apotheosis of contradiction. They proved that God didn't exist, and that God did exist. This small Prussian professor as a philosopher was far from small, and as a leader of the far-reaching German speculation was severely bold. Quite in keeping with the indulgent custom of the philosophic guild, his earlier work contradicts his later theses, and he ultimately believed that his beliefs were past believing. But leaving the philosophical jetsam for the philosopher to salvage, let us dredge for some of the precious scientific treasures in the Cosmogony—treasures especially valuable for their historical significance. It is refreshing to find how stupid we are to have advanced so little in fifteen decades. Perhaps a century hence even some of our fatuous guesses will be fished up and kindly wondered at.

In science Kant paid the usual penalty of thinking faster, further, and deeper than the mob, for the mob just ignored him. To this day the scientist generally recognizes him as a vague classic in philosophy and therefore best left alone. The ground he had covered in *The Universal Natural History and Theory of the Heavens* was later unknowingly worked by others. His concept of the Milky Way as a World of Worlds subsequently became current doctrine. A part of his cosmogony mightily influenced the scientific thinking of the nineteenth century, but under the name of Laplace's Nebular Hypothesis. Kant was, moreover, a thoroughgoing pre-organic evolutionist a century before Wallace and Darwin in 1859 presented suggestions at that epochal meeting of a London scientific society.

The *Natural History of the Heavens* was published in 1755 when Laplace, aged six years, was quite innocent of designs on cosmic gases and dust; but Kant's publisher failed, and for years the *Natural History* collected the dust of that part of the cosmos that surrounded Peterson's ill-fated printery. When later the book was dug up and parts of it reprinted, Kant was already a leader in philosophic thought and a groper in metaphysical mists, and then, as now, little attention was paid to the scientific contributions of a metaphysician.

We might be inclined to mourn over the general neglect of Kant's remarkable cosmogonic contribution, except for two reasons. In the first place he had predecessors who are equally, or even more, neglected by the hurried and harassed scientist of the present day; and in the second place he made some wild guesses that deserve neglect. Both Thomas Wright, of England, and one of the famous scientific Cassini family in France preceded Kant and excelled him in the speculations concerning the rings of Saturn. These two predecessors considered the rings composed of myriads of moonlets; but Kant attributed them to vaporous exhalations from the planet, and was led to an ingenious but erroneous calculation of their periods of rotation. Wright also anticipated Kant in his speculations on the structure of the Milky Way. In fact it was Wright's published letters on the subject, summarized in a Hamburg newspaper, that set Kant's fertile imagination in action and produced the general cosmogony which deals not only with the Milky Way problem, but with the origin of stars and of planetary systems, the death of worlds, the diffusion of life, and all the imaginable processes from those concealed in the original material chaos of the primordial nebula to those of the present mental chaos of the inquiring human being.

Despite his daring and mental freedom, Kant was visibly hampered, as was Thomas Wright before him, with traces of inherited orthodoxy. He

needs must square planetary and stellar phenomena with Infinite Wisdom and Goodness. A
Wise Creator and a Supreme Being forever haunt
his mathematics and astronomy. If a modern in-
vestigator uses such terms or their less compromis-
ing equivalents, he is likely at least to leave off the
capitals; but you may be sure that his doubts or
irreverence never lead him to neglect to capitalize
a certain personal pronoun.

The writer on cosmogony is always impressed
with the religious aspect of his subject. Kant pref-
aces his *Universal Natural History and Theory
of the Heavens* with a sort of apologetic essay on
Religion and Science. He wants it to appear clear
that his thoughts lack no reverence, although he
has been led to adopt, in part, the theories of soul-
less epicurean philosophers. Apparently as a pre-
caution, he did not attach his name to the book,
though his long, devout preface would seem to protect him in his superficially unworthy views. Kant
realized, even better than most of us do today, that
religion and science in the last analysis are the
same. The science of yesterday is the revealed religion of today, and the science revealed today will
be the religion of tomorrow. But the religion we
are speaking of here has nothing whatever to do
with orthodoxy. It has nothing to do with such

things as Methodism, Catholicism, or Calvinism. Except, of course, in practice.

Kant's great scientific synthesis touched on so many phases of cosmogony which are of present-day interest that only a few items can be isolated for discussion in this essay. We shall contrast his pregnant suggestions concerning the origin of the planets, the nature of nebulæ, the center of the universe, and the shortening of the day, with our modern views on these subjects. But we should first mention that Kant also treated with astonishing insight such subjects as the zodiacal light, the aging of the Earth, the motions of stars (not yet then certainly observed), the nature of comets, and the maintenance of the heat of the Sun. In some places errors crept in and deductions were made that we now call erroneous; but Kant labelled many of these portions as dangerously speculative. They were not worthy, he said, of comparison with the deductions based on direct observation and the highly reverenced laws of Newton. In fact, the more fanciful parts were suppressed by him in a later edition.

To account for the origin of the solar system one nebular hypothesis was proposed by Kant; another was devised forty years later by Laplace, the prince of French mathematicians. Both are based on Newtonian mechanics; both derive the planetary system from a primitive nebula, which is the source of the materials and of the motions of the individual bodies. Beyond this point there is little or no similarity between the two nebular hypotheses, though they are frequently confused. There can be little doubt but that Kant's conception is better able to withstand the criticism of modern astronomical research. According to our present view, however, neither scheme of planetary origin can be maintained. We are now inclined to derive Sun and planets at different epochs in the life history of a sidereal body, and not to generate them simultaneously from a contracting primordial nebula, as Kant and Laplace imagined. Both of these early cosmogonists were inspired to their theories of the origin of the planets through contemplation of Saturn and his flat system of rings and satellites. The families of Saturn and of Jupiter closely resemble the solar family on a reduced scale. The cosmic process that forms one type of system was then and is now naturally appealed to in the interpretation of the other. Gravitation is undoubtedly the master key to nearly all the cosmic locks; but alas! much darkness still prevails, and in our befuddled condition many keyholes evade our clumsy groping. The secret, for instance, of the origin of Saturn's rings is not yet unlocked.

The nebular hypotheses of the eighteenth century had the following remarkable observational facts as the basis for theoretical consideration: (1) The planets all move in the same direction around the Sun and in nearly the same plane; (2) The moons of the various planets (in so far as known at that time) move in the same direction as the planets; (3) The motions of rotation of planets and Sun are in the same direction as the motions in the orbits,—that is, counter-clockwise as seen from the north pole; (4) The orbits of the planets and satellites are nearly circular, though the paths followed by comets have great eccentricities.

To account for these facts the great French mathematician proposed, somewhat timorously, that the Sun was formerly an immense fiery nebulous mass, slowly rotating about an axis. The whirling hot mass would tend to lose energy through radiation into the coldness of surrounding space. As a result of the cooling-off, the gaseous mass would shrink, and in accordance with a fundamental principle of mechanics, the speed of rotation would increase. This basic principle of the "conservation of angular momentum" requires that the product of the mass *times* the speed *times* the average distance of the particles from the center should remain constant; and when the distance decreases through shrinkage, the speed of rotation must progressively increase to maintain the constancy of the product, for the mass is essentially invariable. Laplace envisaged the shrinking process going on to such an extent with the passage of time that the speed of rotation became disruptively high. He believed that, when the centrifugal force that goes with rotation balanced the gravitative control of the central part of the rotating nebula, a ring of matter would be detached which no longer partakes in the acceleration of rotation as the nebulous sun further contracts. We are all familiar with the Laplacian idea that the material in each ring ultimately condensed into a planet, but we are less acquainted with the objections to the Laplacian hypotheses that have been raised by numerous students of the problem. For instance, the formation of the rings in the manner supposed is physically impossible, though subsidiary hypotheses can be advanced to circumvent this objection. Moreover, a ring once formed could not give birth to a large planet, widely separated from other planets, but would condense into multitudes of very small planets, if condensation of any sort were possible. The planets born of such rings should rotate backward instead of forward, unless further protective hypotheses are introduced. The rings of Saturn and a satellite of Mars both turn more rapidly than the hypothesis allows. Finally, the motions of those satellites of Uranus, Neptune, Jupiter, and Saturn, subsequently discovered, present examples of retrograde, clockwise, motions that require further patching of the theory, or its abandonment.

Kant's hypothesis fares much better with these criticisms, probably because it is more elastic and adaptable. But a prime advantage is its meteoric character, which frees it from the supposition of a hot gas, rotating as a unit and casting off rings. In attempting to make his hypothesis extremely general and applicable to the universe as a whole, Kant made the error of assuming that the primordial solar nebula was at rest, originally, and obtained its existing angular momentum through the relative motions of its individual parts. That cannot be done. Since some original condition must be assumed, it is simplest, as Laplace foresaw, to assume original rotation rather than rest.

Laplace, we recall, dealt only with the solar system. Newton, likewise, did not extend his analyses to the stellar system, for which little observational material was then available. Wright and Lambert, both contemporaries of Kant, confined their speculations mainly to the Milky Way. But Kant included all, solar system and Galaxy, moons and nebulæ. Equipped with practically all of the science of his day, with a constructive imagination and literary pen, he sought to interpret the solar system as one of myriads. He boldly attempted to correlate moral and physical law, to write the first great epic of cosmic evolution and a scientific Book of Genesis.

Philosophers glory in the sweep of such a universal speculation. They hold it as a sign of Kant's eminence and strength that he attempted to interpret the workings of the whole cosmos. Scientists are prone to hold the same quality as a sign of weakness—this extrapolating. so far beyond the tangible facts.

One is tempted to grieve with Helmholtz that Kant's environment was not propitious for the continuation of his scientific work. If he had had access to such equipment for scientific investigation as we today waste on listless students, it is probable that the world would have lost the *Critiques* and Antinomies. The resulting gain to scientific knowledge, however, might have been incalculable, for Kant was in aptitude and method a natural scientist of the highest order. He could undoubtedly have been in the direct line of cosmic immortals—Copernicus, Kepler, and Newton.

To return to the Kantian nebular hypothesis, we may correct the slip concerning the angular momentum by assuming that the original solar nebula was in rotation, although the total nebulosity for all stars together was, as Kant supposed, momentarily at rest. Back of that original peaceful matter, Kant does not go—he considers it as the first appreciable stage after nothing at all.

Kant's nebula is formed of independent particles, and the development of the planetary system, according to his scheme, partakes of many of the characteristics later developed in Lockyer's meteoritic hypothesis, and still later in the planetesimal theory of Chamberlin and Moulton. He imagined the gravitational formation of a central nucleus, which ultimately becomes the gaseous Sun, and the similar formation of secondary nuclei, which ultimately become the planets, moving in paths in conformance with Newtonian laws. As on some of these points he is not quantitatively specific, the theory easily escapes specific criticism. Probably the most nearly fatal objection is that raised by Harold Jeffreys against all theories, including the planetesimal hypothesis, that suppose the agglomeration, in the gravitational field of the

Sun, of small particles to form the nuclei of growing planets. The velocities impressed on such particles by the dominating solar mass are so great that, in general, collisions must vaporize the material of colliding bodies, and the planetesimal masses being relatively small, the vapors would forthwith diffuse into space.

I believe it would still be possible to fit the Kantian hypothesis to the facts of modern observational astronomy without much alteration, providing we assume in the primordial solar nebula not only the requisite rotation but well-advanced primary and secondary nuclei. But that device is merely placing the problem unexplained back into the nebula.

The present tidal evolution theory of the origin of the solar system bears little resemblance to either of the nebular hypotheses. It represents not only a drastic step in the attempt to harmonize observational data in astronomy and geology and the theoretical demands of mathematical physics, but it seems to me to signify an advance of considerable philosophic import. In brief, the theory derives the planets catastrophically from the atmosphere of the Sun, the encounter of the Sun with another star being the source of tidal disruption. The birth of a planetary system therefore becomes not the natural course of events in the contractional life history of every star, but it appears as a sporadic adventure. The disaster that results in the formation of planets is not necessarily associated with the early history of the star; it may occur early or late in the stellar career, and many times or none; but the final result obviously will depend upon the physical conditions of the bodies involved, and the nature of the encounter. When we observe that the separation of the stars in space is so wide that, even with their remarkably high velocities, suitable encounters could occur but once in millions of millions of years, we grasp the philosophic bearing of the problem. It leads directly to astonishing conceptions of time and space, and to futile reasonings on infinities and eternities, and on first origins and final causes.

The tidal evolution theory first appeared a quarter of a century ago under the name of the planetesimal hypothesis. The originators, Chamberlin and Moulton, of Chicago, have failed to convince either geologists or astronomers of the necessity of two of the features originally proposed, the connection of planetary systems with spiral nebulæ, and the construction of planets piecemeal out of planetesimals or meteoritic fragments. The spiral nebulæ are suggestive of disruption, to be sure, but it is now considered that beyond that suggestion their relevance ceases. The idea of infalling planetesimals opposes the idea of an originally molten Earth of practically present dimensions—an idea which many geologists believe is necessitated by the complicated and profuse evidences of the rocks. Various students have suggested modifications of the tidal theory, and especially Jeans and Jeffreys have carried through highly suggestive theoretical analyses of the problem.

One point stands out clearly. The origin of our planetary system through the encounter of the Sun with another body requires very special conditions in order that the gravitatively formed tide in the gaseous atmosphere of the Sun should produce the planets as we now find them. And we must assume that, since the passage of this now unknown progenitor, no other encounter has ensued to wreck the delicately poised planetary system. The evidence of the terrestrial rocks shows that a thousand million years at least have elapsed since the tidal eruption that started us off. There are some suggestions in this situation that would have been productively fascinating to the little professor at Königsberg.

It appears that Kant's nebular hypothesis cannot well withstand present-day criticism. The same is discouragingly true of his suggestion that Sirius may be the central body of the stellar system. Also, his suggestion that spiral nebulæ are other galactic systems does not meet universal acceptance. But his theory that tidal friction is slowing down the rotation of the Earth stands accepted. He was undoubtedly the first to point out this important factor of tidal action, and he went even further to explain that in the early history of the Moon its tides, caused by the Earth's attraction, had resulted in reducing lunar rotation and revolution to the same period, forever holding one face of the Moon toward the Earth. These tidal matters were discussed even before the *Natural History of the Heavens* was published, but they appeared only in a Königsberg newspaper, with the result that the important deductions had to be independently discovered by several different investigators during the next century.

In conclusion we note that Kant was the first to insist on the "island universe" interpretation of nebulæ, and his arguments are practically the same as those used by modern proponents of the theory that celestial spirals are other galaxies like our own. He also proposed the modern theory that the Sun is north of the plane of the Milky Way, and that it probably is well off the axis through the center. Thomas Wright also maintained these views in part, but he placed a weird material god at the center of the universe and involved his whole conception in exaggerated and ridiculous fancy. Kant, on the other hand, although always painfully aware of an overlording supreme intelligence, followed his speculations concerning galactic structure and planetary origin with precise logic and inspired literary expression. The celestial problem is indeed one of unrivalled sublimity, appealing equally to scientific precision and boundless imagination. It always succeeds in inspiring the sincerest efforts of its devotees.

ART

KUNO FRANCKE

THERE is a curious anomaly, a streak of paradoxical antagonism between the inner and the outer, between essence and form, running through all of Kant's life and work. On the one hand, a scholastic existence as isolated and circumscribed as only the public conditions of continental Europe in the eighteenth century under the sway of princely absolutism could make it; on the other, a breadth and sweep of intellectual interest transcending all boundaries. On the one hand, a subject dutifully submitting to autocratic power in State and Church; on the other, a thinker revolutionizing the whole view of the universe. On the one hand, a rigid formalist, a meticulous adherent to technical terms and hairsplitting definitions; on the other, an inspired seer and prophet. Although the most momentous manifestation of this paradox is to be seen in the metaphysical, moral, religious, and political phases of Kant's activity, it comes out no less strikingly in his contributions to the theory of art.

Limited as he was throughout his life to the

narrow confines of the neighborhood of his native town of Königsberg, in a province far removed from the great art centers of the national past, he never had an opportunity of seeing the great monuments of mediæval architecture, sculpture or painting in other parts of the Fatherland; and if he had seen them, he would, as an advocate of classicist formalism, probably have ignored them. His intense rationalism kept him entirely aloof from the Romantic revival in German literature that set in with the Storm and Stress movement. He had no understanding for the beauty of the classic days of Weimar and Jena. Of all his works, his treatise on æsthetics—the *Kritik der Urteils-kraft*—is perhaps the worst in style; and parts of it are veritable orgies of abstruseness and be-wildering scholastic nomenclature. And yet, this thoroughly inartistic, unemotional, and sensu-ously obtuse man has, in æsthetics also, by sheer power of reasoning, made discoveries which pre-sent the nature and aim of all art in a new light. What are these discoveries?

First. In consonance with the subjective tenor of his whole philosophy, Kant saw in beauty not an inherent and fixed quality of things, but a par-ticular form of the reaction of the human mind upon impressions received from within or without.

And in accordance with the distinctly spiritual character of his whole philosophy, he limited the use of the term beauty to such reactions as tend to strengthen and heighten the spiritual nature of man.

From this point of view, secondly, it becomes a matter of irrelevance whether the object which arouses the feeling of the beautiful exists in reality or not. Indeed, the further it is removed from association with actual existence, the greater its spiritual appeal is bound to be. The more—thus we may perhaps illustrate Kant's thought—the more in the contemplation of a sunset we forget the actual conditions about us, the hill on which we stand, the details of the scenery before us, farms, forests, river courses, the more the immensity of space, outline, and color before us assumes for us the form of a Fata Morgana of the imagination, the deeper will our enjoyment be. The more a lyric poem, a symphony, a drama transports us into the region of the timeless, the infinite, the universal, the firmer will be its hold upon our innermost soul. And is it not true that the life of a beloved one acquires its fullest meaning for us only after it has departed, so that we can look at it detached from all reality, as a complete unit, a thing of beauty, raised above the world of fleeting appearances?

Here we touch upon the third of Kant's contributions to æsthetics: absence of desire is of the very essence of æsthetic enjoyment. Other pleasurable emotions are closely interwoven with desire. The sensuously agreeable arouses our desire for possession of the agreeable object. The morally good arouses our desire for its attainment. The æsthetically beautiful alone, partaking as it does both of the sensuous and the moral nature of man, gives a sense of complete satisfaction, of complete harmony of all our faculties, and sinks all desire in the mere joy of contemplation and the feeling of evenly balanced free strength. The beautiful, in other words, redeems us from the conflicts of the will, it stills the passions, it restores man to full mastery of self, to the free play of his powers, to what with a slight modification of Kant's phraseology might be called "purposefulness without purpose." "Only when he plays, man is fully man" —this word of Kant's great pupil Schiller epigrammatically expresses wherein Kant saw the liberating effect of the beautiful.

Another æsthetically basic feeling is the sense of the sublime. This feeling also is conceived of by Kant as an act of spiritual self-delivery. As beings of the senses, we are anything but uplifted by what forces itself upon us as gigantic, colossal, or

unmeasurable. The sight of the limitless ocean or
the vast solitude of the desert, the experience of a
violent thunderstorm or the eruption of a volcano,
have at first a depressing or a terrifying effect
upon us. We feel our littleness, our weakness and
helplessness face to face with such vast dimensions and such tremendous forces. But soon a de-
fense reaction—to use a modern term—sets in, our
spiritual nature asserts itself. We feel ourselves a
part of the living spirit that pervades this infinite
space and sets in motion these wonderful revolutions of nature. We feel an active power in us akin
to the life of the portentous phenomena before us.
And thus we are enabled to transform the overwhelming sensations of terror and awe into the
feeling of the sublime, that is, to raise ourselves to
the level of the object of our sensations and see in
it a manifestation of the life that assures our own
spiritual sublimity.

The mission of art, then,—this is the point
toward which all these considerations tend—the
mission of art, according to Kant, is to release
these powers of the spirit, to give man his true
inner freedom. This task can be accomplished
only if art produces without conscious effort, without any specific aim as to the content of its pro-
ductions, guided solely by the instinct for pure

form, that is, the organic unity of all the parts constituting a whole. This is the way in which nature produces; this is why nature, unless checked by destructive forces, produces nothing but æsthetically satisfying forms. In a like manner, the artistic genius, if unencumbered by motives alien to the formative instinct—such as the appeal to vulgar appetites, the desire to startle, the desire to teach—cannot fail to produce forms æsthetically satisfying. In Kant's own words: "nature is beautiful when she appears as art; art is beautiful when she appears as nature."

Such are some of the fundamental ideas by which Kant has become the father of modern æsthetics. That he should have arrived at them without any æsthetic experiences of his own, in surroundings barren of artistic influences, unaided by any sort of psychological experimentation, solely through abstract reasoning, is indeed a striking proof of his speculative genius. It will be a gain to humanity, if these ideas, differently formulated perhaps and adapted to the needs of our own day, continue to be a motive power, not only in the theories of art, but also in art itself.

LAW

ROSCOE POUND

NO philosopher, unless it be Aristotle, has left so deep an impress upon the science of law as has Immanuel Kant. Kant marks an epoch in philosophical jurisprudence. He struck a decisive blow at the philosophical science of law which had obtained for the past two centuries, and laid out the path for philosophy of law in the nineteenth century. Until Kant, jurisprudence was rested upon a theory of natural rights which were either inherent moral qualities of man in a state of abstract perfection or deductions from a social compact expressing the nature of the perfect abstract man. But if natural rights were inherent moral qualities, to be ascertained by reason, granting that reason could deduce infallibly from given premises, how could reason give us the premises? And if natural rights were grounded on a social compact, how could the details or the implied terms of a compact made in the remote past bind each and all of us today? The fiction of representation, a political application of the legal conception of mandate or agency, on the basis whereof Blackstone could argue that we are bound because we were represented when our forefathers made the contract, was suggested obviously by the British political theory in which all are taken to consent to acts of Parliament through the representatives sent to Westminster to act for them. Such a basis for the authority of the legal order could not stand criticism. Kant sought to find the basis of rights and of the securing of rights by the legal order in some ultimate datum which might afford an un-challengeable foundation. He found this funda-mental datum in the individual free will. He con-ceived that the problem of law was to reconcile potentially conflicting free wills. He held that the principle by which this reconciliation was to be effected was equality in freedom of the will in ac-tion; the application of a universal rule to each ac-tion which would enable the free will of the actor to coexist along with the free will of everyone else. The whole course of juristic thought in the nine-teenth century was determined by this conception. All the nineteenth-century schools in jurispru-dence derive from the resulting breakdown of the classical natural law of the eighteenth century.

Kant's work in the philosophy of law is impor-tant also because of its direct influence upon the historical school, which was dominant in jurisprudence throughout the nineteenth century. A chief juristic problem to Kant and his successors in philosophical jurisprudence was the relation of law to liberty. On the one hand, modern law is characterized by legislation. External restraint and coercion are obvious facts and a philosophy that thinks only of reason and ideal justice is not a philosophy of the law that is. On the other hand, a democratic age, and Kant's *Rechtslehre* speaks from the era of the French Revolution, demands that the legal order have some solid basis other than mere authority and leads the individual to demand the widest possible freedom of action. How were these two ideas, external restraint and individual freedom of action, to be reconciled? Kant met this problem by working out thoroughly the purely judicial notion of justice, the idea of an equal chance to all exactly as they are, to which the individualism of the time and the insistence upon equality in the maturity of law gave such prominence in the juristic thought of the nineteenth century. So he defined right as "the sum of the circumstances according to which the will of one may be reconciled with the will of another according to a common rule of freedom." Savigny, the founder and leader of the historical school in jurisprudence, turned this formula of right into

77

one of law: "The rules whereby the invisible boundaries are determined, within which the existence and activity of each gain secure and free opportunity." If we adhere to an idealistic interpretation of legal history, thinking of the development of law as a gradual unfolding of Kant's formula of right, this definition is a statement of the position of the historical school. Human experience has gradually discovered how to determine these invisible boundaries and has expressed in rules of law what it has found.

Nor is Kant's influence upon the historical jurists confined to the general theory. It may be traced in details on all sides. To give but two examples, Savigny's theory of possession, one of the enduring achievements of his school, manifestly builds upon Kant's theory of acquisition. Indeed he seeks to put the law of possession in terms of that theory, and to apply to the texts of the Roman law the difficulties that Kant raises and seeks to solve in his discussion of the philosophy of property. Again Kant's discussion of supervening hardship in case of change in the value of currency is the basis of a discussion of the provisions of the Prussian code in Savigny's treatise on obligations. Next to the historical school the group of most importance in the legal science of the last century was the English analytical school. John Austin, the founder and leader of this school, was a disciple of Bentham. But the institutional treatises which he had studied in Germany were Kantian in their philosophy, and Austin had read Kant and kept Kant's writings upon the philosophy of law and morals among his books. The effect of this may be seen in more than one place in Austin's lectures and is notable in his theory of the relation of law and morals, which is often rated among his principal achievements.

What is more important, Kant summed up the idea of the end of law, which obtained from the seventeenth to the nineteenth century, in what seems its final statement. From one standpoint or another all the nineteenth-century schools came to one result as to the end of the legal order, and that result is best expressed in Kant's formula. Nineteenth-century metaphysical jurisprudence developed the idea of free will into the practical consequence of liberty, an idea of general freedom of action for individuals. Hence the end of law was to secure to each individual the widest possible liberty. Though Anglo-American jurists professed to pay little or no attention to the systems of the metaphysical school, its central idea of a maximum of free individual abstract self-assertion had decisive influence in many parts of the law, and still affects the orthodox doctrine as to liability for tort and American decisions as to what is due process of law. Again Sir Henry Maine's famous generalization that the development of law is a progress from status to contract puts the same idea concretely in terms of legal institutions. It finds the end of law in liberty, conceived of as the widest possible individual self-assertion. It teaches that a movement from individual subjection to individual freedom is the key to social and hence to legal development. It takes the maximum of abstract individual self-assertion to be the maximum realization of the idea of liberty. Hence legal progress is a progress from institutions wherein rights, duties, and liabilities are annexed to status or relation to one where rights, duties, and liabilities flow from voluntary action and are consequences of exertion of the human will. The direction of legal development is realizing Kant's formula.

It is in no wise different when we turn from the metaphysical and the historical jurists to other nineteenth-century schools. Thus, Spencer's formula of justice is a Kantian formula. Spencer had never read Kant. But Kant had become part of the thought of the time so thoroughly that each of the significant schools—the metaphysical school, the historical school, the later English utilitarians, and the positivists—came to his position, although for different reasons and in different ways. Even the economic realists who arose late in the century, sought an abstract individual liberty through collective action and sought a maximum of governmental control as a means to a maximum of liberty.

But Kant's influence endures beyond the legal science of the nineteenth century and is no less marked in the newer schools that characterize the legal science of today. The Neo-Kantians were the first to challenge the supremacy of the historical school at the end of the nineteenth century. They have been leaders in the revival of philosophical jurisprudence and the supplanting of the juristic pessimism of the immediate past by a renewed juridical idealism, which are remaking the science of law today. Kant's conception of the legal order as a reconciling or harmonizing of wills in action by means of universal rules becomes in the hands of the social utilitarian a compromise or adjustment of advantages, a balance of interests. In the hands of economic realists it becomes a reconciling or harmonizing of wants—"the satisfaction of every one's wants so far as they are not outweighed by others' wants." In the hands of the positivist sociologists it becomes an adjustment of social functions. In the hands of psychological sociologists it becomes a reconciling or harmonizing or adjusting of claims or demands or desires. In all forms of the social philosophical jurisprudence of today, Kant's statement of the task of the legal order as one of reconciling, harmonizing or adjusting by means of a universal rule, may be seen in the background.

There are, perhaps, two reasons for Kant's enduring influence upon jurisprudence. In the first place, he saw the fundamental philosophical difficulties of a science of law and put its persistent problems in a way that compels us to recur to him. Secondly, he saw and thought through the difficulties involved in our attempts to solve these problems, so that our endeavors toward new solutions cannot dispense with a study of his, whereby, if nothing else, we may learn the obstacles with which all such endeavors must contend.

PEACE

GERHART VON SCHULZE-GAEVERNITZ

T
HE peace conception of Kant[1] is not the
hobby of an old man, but the ripest fruit of
his philosophy based upon two of his fundamental
ideas: freedom and mankind. Kant's philosophy
has been called the watershed of the times: his
peace conception sums up the past and points to
the future; it is distinctly modern.

The postulate of *freedom* leads to the conception of an ideal state of society, which might be
described thus: Man has mastered nature, as a
means to his own purposes. But no man is used as
a means; everyone is an end in himself. Therefore, the freedom of the one is limited only in
order to allow the freedom of others. Each individual's aims include the reasonable aims of his
fellows; he does not seek only his own good, but
that of his neighbors as well. In this stage of society there is no compulsion; morality reigns. War,

---

[1] Kant, *Zum ewigen Frieden*. Königsberg, 1795. 50
pages. Translated by W. Hastie: *Eternal Peace and other
International Essays* by Immanuel Kant, Boston, World
Peace Foundation, 1914.

as the most brutal form of compulsion, is abandoned. Kant objects to war, not because it means suffering, but because it means constraint. In this respect he has become the heir of the Puritans and the Quakers, and follows the word of the Apostle: "Ye are called to liberty."

Another line of thought leads to the same result. The human race should be viewed as an historic whole which emerged from nature to build up civilization, from necessity to work out freedom. Only through *mankind* as an historic unit, can man hope to attain his destination, whereas an individual animal, if perfectly developed, can reach such perfection as is attainable by the species. Human history is a system, with a regular movement toward progress. In this evolution, he maintains, *war* has played and plays still an important rôle. Even costly armaments may induce the princes to favor commercial and industrial enterprise, and by that, progress. But the more humanity becomes conscious of its unity, the more war is incompatible with this unity because it produces dissension where there ought to be cooperation. Kant likes to exemplify with economic arguments the word of the Apostle: "Where one member suffers, all members suffer." A wrong done in one place is felt all over the globe, when world economics have become as interlaced as they are in modern times.

Both concepts lead to the idea of a perfect human society as the goal of all history, a society which, in religious terms, might be described as the "kingdom of heaven." This ideal is to be striven for on this earth, but to be realized only in the Transcendental. Not so with Kant's peace conception. This is a concrete terrestrial proposal. There is a real danger that popular interpretation will regard this idea, too, as transcendental—only to be realized in an unattainable future—and so reduce it to the commonplace, "Peace is to come when all men have become angels." This misconception prevailed in Germany during the last generation, even with Windelband.

To avoid this danger, let us remember the fundamental distinction between morality and legality. Just because man is bad, he must be forced by the law, to legal action, if not to moral disposition. Quite the same principle applies to states which follow their selfish aims by robbery and treachery at the expense of other states. They must be kept in check by a universal constitution, an international federation, a "world union," which will make international law as peremptory as national law. To a union of states "conjoined with power" every member state must submit. This is a terrestrial, not a transcendental, task; a judicial conception, not an ethical one. Such a "world union," Kant assures us repeatedly, is attainable as a fact, and is destined to supersede the practice of falsely so-called treaties of peace. The commercial spirit and the power of money work in the same direction. Kant says, perhaps too optimistically, that they cannot exist along with war, and that they will sooner or later control every people.

The means recommended by Kant to promote his peace conception are of a legal nature. First of all, the members of the peace federation are to have republican constitutions. Especially, the decision whether there is to be war or not ought to fall to the people, and not to a sovereign who, if he decides for war, does not have to give up his pleasures and palaces. They will decide, Kant hopes, for durable peace, since they are the sufferers from war. The federation which Kant advocates means a republic of free states, small and large, on equal terms, not the overwhelming power of one state that has overgrown the rest. The freedom of the member states requires that no state shall meddle by force with the inner policy of another. Standing armies are to be abolished, and no debts contracted for armament. It is clear that this whole plan is not an ideal, but a vehicle to the ideal. Kant once said that even "a race of devils" could be brought to live in peace by a law rightly conceived and strictly enforced.

He admits that his peace plan can be realized by only one step at a time. Even if we suppose that by a federation of the progressive states, war is outlawed, men will not live in paradise. There remain competition and exploitation of men by men, land rents and monopolies,—problems to be worked out by reason. But, in any case, the establishment of a peace order means a decisive step toward the "cultural unity of mankind" which Kant sharply distinguishes from the peace federation. The former means an ideal state in which mankind has developed all the capacities inherent in man. "From step to step shalt thou go, commencing with the single man and his education. Thou shalt first place him under the idea of duty, then proceed to the lawful ordering of thine own nation, then to the federation of all nations, and then to the cultural unity of the whole world."

For the fulfilment of his plan, Kant hopes that some powerful and enlightened people will form themselves into a republic as, in 1795 when he wrote his essay, America was doing under Washington's administration. It is known how much he sympathized with the American Revolution. He also felt keen sympathy with the French Revolution. He hoped that some such strong and neutral republic would furnish a center of federative union for other states, and that such a union would extend more and more widely. So Kant points to America's world mission. So President Eliot in his book *A Late Harvest* urges America to take the lead in the federation of the world. Kant more than a century ago in a marvelous way formulated the best traditions and highest aspirations of America. Let our motto be, "Forward with Kant."